THE ORVIS®

STREAMSIDE GUIDE TO

APPROACH AND PRESENTATION

Riffles, Runs, Pocket Water, and Much More

Tom Rosenbauer

Illustrations by Rod Walinchus
Photographs by Tom Rosenbauer

SKYHORSE PUBLISHING

Skyhorse Publishing books may be purchased in bulk at special discounts for sales promotion, corporate gifts, fund-raising, or educational purposes. Special editions can also be created to specifications. For details, contact the Special Sales Department, Skyhorse Publishing, 307 West 36th Street, 11th Floor, New York, NY 10018 or info@skyhorsepublishing.com.

Skyhorse® and Skyhorse Publishing® are registered trademarks of Skyhorse Publishing, Inc.®, a Delaware corporation.

Visit our website at www.skyhorsepublishing.com.

10 9 8 7 6 5 4 3 2

Library of Congress Cataloging-in-Publication Data

Rosenbauer, Tom.
  The Orvis guide to approach and presentation / Tom Rosenbauer.
      pages cm
  Includes index.
  ISBN 978-1-62087-620-6
  1. Fly fishing--Technique. I. Title.
  SH456.R663 2013
  799.12'4--dc23

                                        2012050552

ISBN: 978-1-62087-620-6

Printed in China

Contents

Acknowledgments

TO ALL THOSE FRIENDS WHO HAVE KINDLY shown me their secret spots and tricks, thank you. Over the years, I've learned especially valuable streamcraft from Bob Bachman, Mark, Joe, and the late Vern Bressler; Monroe Coleman, Rick and Patty Eck, Todd and J.T. France, Dick Galland, Kevin Gregory, Steve Herter, Pat McCord, Jim McFadyean, Craig Matthews, Neil Ringler, Paul Roos, and Ed Schroeder.

Introduction

YOU'VE POLISHED YOUR CASTING AFTER attending a flyfishing school or spending hours with a patient mentor. You've practiced your knots. Last summer, you floated a Montana River with a guide, catching plenty of trout when he told you just where to cast and when to mend your line. You have a basic knowledge of flies. Now comes the true test for any fly fisher: exploring an unknown river by yourself with no one to give you advice, spot the fish, or tell you whether to fish the pools or riffles. You are not a complete fly fisher until you can do this.

I hope this book will be a helpful friend, a guide to uncharted waters, a reference to fall back on each time you fish new rivers. If you learn the lessons in this book, and if you are observant, I think you will find that fishing new rivers and streams will be easy and fun, and you'll take great pride in your newfound expertise.

I'm not suggesting that you'll know it all if you memorize everything in this book and fish a half-dozen rivers. The best fly fishers will tell you they learn something new every time they fish, and if you don't keep looking for those fresh nuggets you'll be fooling yourself and missing out on many of the pleasures of fly fishing.

This guide is a distillation of what I have learned in over 35 years of fishing, observing, and most important, listening and watching other anglers and guides on the water. I am sure that between the time I deliver this manuscript to Jay Cassell and Nick Lyons, my editors, and the time the book is printed I will have learned a score of new insights on trout behavior, tactics for presenting a fly, three new ways to fish a nymph, and a new way of fishing streamers. The next river you fish could contradict much of what I say in this book and throw all of my smug theories into the trash. I hope you agree that's what makes fly fishing so intriguing!

1

Planning Your Day

SOMETIMES YOU CAN JUMP INTO A RIVER with both feet while the engine of your car is still ticking and catch trout right off the bat, without a moment's hesitation for planning. But don't count on it. The best fishing trips are ones you've prepared for. You have probably

Even on popular rivers like Montana's Madison, you can find solitude if you're willing to walk.

spent days or weeks getting your tackle in order, tying flies, cleaning lines, or building leaders. You have planned your route by car or airplane, and have arranged for someplace to stay. In order to get the most fun out of any fishing trip, whether it's for a week's vacation or just a few hours after work, you'll be more successful and take more pride in your skills with some planning and observation.

First, check the Internet, books, or the closest reliable fly shop for stream conditions and where the best fishing will be found. On most of our rivers, the best spots have already been found and there will be some record of them. Get a map of the river—most of our more popular rivers are detailed in special fishing maps that you can buy in a fly shop, copy from a book, or download from the Internet. Barring that, get a U.S. Geological Survey (USGS) topographic map of the area (the new CD-ROMS that include all the topo maps for a state are terrific). If you don't like crowds, check the map and find places near the supposed hot spots where you might have to walk a mile away from a parking area. Most fly fishers today are reluctant to walk more than a few hundred yards from their vehicles, and some actually seem to enjoy fishing in crowds. I don't. And I have found solitude on some of our most famous and crowded trout streams, from the South Platte in Colorado to the Beaverkill in New York to the Bighorn in Montana.

I don't always get to fish the prime water, and I might see fewer fish than I would in the more famous pools, but I enjoy the experience more.

Don't stop at the first parking place you see. Drive up and down the river and see where most of the anglers are and what the water looks like. Stop at bridges to see the river at different spots. Sometimes a river that looks too shallow in one place will have lots of fine runs 100 yards away. After a rainstorm, a river might look dirty in one place, but after driving upstream you'll see a muddy tribu-

Spending time on the bank before jumping into the water can improve your chances of a successful day.

tary entering the river and find that the water is crystal clear upstream of where the tributary enters. Many times insects will hatch in one place in a river and not others; during the famous salmonfly hatch of the Rockies, for example, the huge stoneflies will hatch in only a short stretch of a river for a few days and will gradually work upstream over a period of two weeks. By doing a little reconnaissance you might be lucky enough to hit this hatch at the prime time and follow its progression up the river.

I'm not suggesting that you play tourist all day long. Once you've decided where you'd like to fish, load the camera with film, grab a bottle of water and a few munchies, and head to the river for the rest of the day. If you might miss dinner, take a flashlight in case you decide to stay for the evening hatch.

HOW TO OBSERVE THE WATER

It's a good idea to get the Big Picture of a river before you start fishing. The best place is a bridge, where you can see both banks upstream and downstream. And the best thing that can happen is that you see fish rising all over the place. In this instance, all you need to do is determine where the bigger fish are feeding and spot a place where no one else is fishing. Ninety-nine times out of 100 you won't be so lucky.

Look for depth and current speed first. Where are the places more than two feet deep with a moderate current, places where trout have the security of depth yet a current fast enough to bring them a steady supply of food? Is there deep water near the bank, where trout can hide under overhanging vegetation? Or is all the best water out in the middle of the river? Is the water muddy or clear? Your approach and presentation should be chosen based on water clarity. Look at the banks. Streamside grass that is under water indicates that a river is higher than normal; wide dry banks tell you the river is probably lower than normal. Is the river bottom composed of sand, gravel, big rocks, or aquatic weed? All of these things can tell you where the fish will be found and what techniques to use, as you'll find later in this book.

Now climb down the bank and take the water temperature. Trout are cold-blooded, and how they feed is often determined by how far the water temperature varies from that perfect 60 to 63°F mark. Turn over a few rocks to see what kind of insect life is present. Shake a few streamside trees or bushes to see if any insects have hatched recently.

2

How to Enter a Pool

WHAT HAPPENS WHEN A TROUT IS FRIGHTENED

MORE TROUT ARE NOT CAUGHT BY ANGLERS because they are frightened than for any other reason. A trout gets frightened in degrees: a splash in the water 50 feet away, pulsed through the water to a trout's lateral line, may put the fish on alert. This fish will stop feeding for a minute or so, and if the disturbance does not return, the fish will resume feeding. Another splash or a line falling over the trout's head is likely to make the fish settle to the bottom, close to a rock or log and nearly out of sight. This fish might not feed for 10 or 15 minutes. An angler walking near the fish, a big shadow falling over its position, or a rock thrown into the river will make the fish bolt for a safe place—and this fish might not feed again for a full day.

This angler was only trying to capture a sample of a
hatching mayfly, but the ripples made by his wading
might spook every fish in the pool.

You can never predict how closely you can approach a trout without spooking it, because each fish has a different personality and conditions change every day. In general, trout can be approached easily when:

- The river you are fishing has an abundance of food and trout feed frequently
- The water is dirty enough so that you can't see your toes in two feet of water
- The fish are lying in water more than five feet deep
- The weather is dark and rainy
- It is before dawn or after sunset
- Trout are holding in fast riffled water where the surface is broken
- The river you are fishing has a constant procession of anglers and boats

Trout are difficult to approach when:

- The water is clear
- There is not much food drifting in the current
- The fish are lying in shallow water
- There is bright sunlight
- The river is fished infrequently
- The surface of the water is smooth

Let me give you an example of extremes. Last April, I thought I would be very clever when fishing the Bighorn in Montana. The trout in this river are not very spooky, because the river has intense angler and boat traffic, lots of riffles, and a bountiful food supply. Even so, I approached the riffle I wanted to fish like a heron—I crawled to the bank and spent the whole morning sitting on the edge of the river, never raising my profile above what would have been waist level had I been standing up. I caught a bunch of fish and felt pretty smug until another angler plopped himself into the riffle on the far side, waded up and down the riffle like a yo-yo, and hooked just as many trout as I did.

On Montana's Bighorn, abundant food and riffled water make for an easy approach because the fish are not spooky.

Then I spent a week in England at a quiet little bed-and-breakfast in a Hampshire village, just a few miles from Orvis UK headquarters. My host owned a tiny chalk stream that ran through his backyard, which he admitted he had never fished, nor had anyone else in recent memory. I dropped a few not-too-subtle hints (I had spotted some very large brown trout in the stream), and finally, at breakfast on my last morning he told me, "I've decided. Fish the stream if you want to, just not close to the path." After leaving the office that day I planned a late afternoon attack. I crept down to the river and spotted several fat trout sipping mayflies in less than a foot of water. I spent a good 15

On the River Itchen in the south of England, clear water and spooky fish mean you have to stay well back from the bank.

minutes watching them, looking over the water as carefully as I could, and entered the tiny stream without making a ripple. I skulked upstream at about an inch per second until I was 30 feet directly behind the lowest fish. My first cast spooked the fish and it made a wake as wide as the little stream, spooking at least five other fish, who joined it in a migration that was soon out of sight, 50 yards around the bend. I cranked up my line and headed for the pub.

THE VALUE OF OBSERVATION

In my experience, wild trout will choose locations in a river where the current brings them constant food, with slower water nearby so they don't exhaust themselves in the process. The best pools in a river are sometimes the closest pools to the road, the closest to parking areas, or under bridges. The trout here may have seen so many anglers and flies that they are crafty as hell, but the best water is the best water regardless of its distance from well-traveled paths. The reason bridge-pool trout are seldom caught is that everyone jumps right into the water, alerting the fish before a cast is ever put over their heads.

Once you have chosen a place to fish, stay well away from the water, either by sitting on the bank or leaning against a big tree or other obstruction. I have spent as long as an hour looking at a pool, but I'm seldom that patient. If you are patient you might see a nice trout feeding right where you were about to slide into the river, and by moving downstream a few yards you might be able to sneak up on that fish and catch it. Watch the water for rising fish and insects on the water. Try to mark the spot of all feeding fish against a couple of landmarks on the bank, because the minute you walk into the water everything will look different.

If you don't see anything rising, mentally fish the pool and try to determine where trout might be lying. This way, you'll hit most of a pool's better spots, some of which might not be as apparent when you get down to water level. On the other hand, some of the places in a pool of riffle might look better or worse when you get close to them while wearing polarized glasses, but at least you've had an overview of the pool.

TAKE A HIKE

Even if you're the most careful angler in the world, once you have fished up through a pool that is less than 20 feet wide you can assume that every trout in the pool has been spooked and won't feed for a while. Trout will be frightened in bigger rivers as well, unless there is deep water that you can't wade through. In the Bighorn, where trout are not spooky, they might start feeding in three minutes. On the other hand, I doubt those trout in the little Hampshire chalk stream ate another mayfly that day.

So by walking beyond the last angler, you will hopefully find trout that will at least look at your fly with interest. On a weekday, you might be able to fish right in the bridge pool; on a weekend, you might have to walk past a dozen pools before you find one that has not been disturbed. I don't always have the luxury, but when I plan on fishing the evening spinner fall on local rivers, I'll drive up and down the river an hour before fishing, looking for an undisturbed pool.

You should also plan your strategy around boat traffic. The pools upstream of canoe and drift boat put-ins will hold trout that aren't disturbed as often. Fish below takeout ramps are also more likely to rise to a dry fly or inhale a nymph later in the day, because most of the boats have left this water hours ago.

3

ANGLE AND ATTITUDE OF APPROACH

HOW MUCH OF YOU CAN A TROUT SEE?

TROUT FACE INTO THE CURRENT. IT'S THE only way they can face because of the way they're built, with bullet-shaped heads in front and a flexible body and tail behind. They feed most often by lying in place, waiting for the current to bring them food. Trout have a blind spot immediately behind them. Unless you splash your line down right on top of them, create ripples on the surface by moving too fast, or make a lot of noise while wading, you can approach them quietly from behind. Be careful in big pools that might have reverse eddies in them, because although you might be facing upstream, the fish may be facing into the current but downstream.

Because of the way water bends light rays, trout can see more of the outside world when lying in a deep pool than they can when lying in shallow water. There are complex formulas and drawings that theorize on just how much a trout can see at various depths. Don't worry about them. Just be aware that a trout in three feet of water can see you from farther away than one lying in a foot of water. You can often keep your body below a trout's window of sight by crouching or kneeling. And by getting into the water and wading close to a trout, rather than approaching one on the bank, you can keep your profile lower.

Your position relative to the sun can make a big difference on bright days. Trout don't have the ability to

Trout facing upstream have a blind spot immediately downstream, and can only see out of the water in a circular window.

squint, so they don't see objects well when looking into
the sun. If the sun is behind your back, a trout will have
a difficult time spotting you unless you let your shadow
fall over a trout's lie, or you are silhouetted against the sky.
Trees or bushes behind you will help break up your profile.
It follows that if you are facing the sun and are illuminated
in bright light, a trout will be able to spot you more easily.
If you have to approach a trout this way, keep your profile
low and your movements slow.

Fly lines flashing in the sun can also spook trout. Use a
side cast to keep the line below their line of sight. False cast
off to the side of a feeding fish and then change direction
on your last cast to get the fly in place. Either that, or make
your false casts deliberately short, shooting enough line on
the last cast to put just your tippet over a trout's head.

SHOULD I FISH UPSTREAM OR DOWN?

Most anglers prefer to move upstream as they fish.
Unless someone is wading just ahead, you'll be coming up
behind trout, where they can't see you as well. The bigger
the stream, the less important this becomes, because once
you get directly across from a fish that's 40 or 50 feet away
it won't be able to see you, or if it does, you won't appear
to be a threat. Still, since most wading fly casters fish dry

flies and nymphs, and both of these methods are best used in an upstream or upstream-and-across direction, it's easier to wade upstream as you fish. If you wade downstream and then turn around the way you came to fish, you are fishing over water that you have just walked through!

In small streams, the direct upstream approach is your best option.

When fishing streamers or wet flies on a swing, it is often easier to work downstream. With these methods you try to cover as much water as possible, so working downstream, wading with the current, tires you less and again lets you present your fly over water you have not yet waded.

On big rivers, with pools that stretch 50 yards or more from bank to bank, sometimes you'll just wade into a pool and fish directly across-current, without moving more than a few yards upstream or downstream. When you're done fishing a spot or a pod of rising fish, you will disturb the water less (and tire yourself less) if you wade back the way you came, walk the bank until you find another spot, and then wade out into the pool. Wading up and down a big pool spoils the water for you and anyone else in the area.

HOW FAST SHOULD I MOVE?

In food-rich streams, full of insect life and fish that don't spook easily, you can hook fish all day long without moving more than a few feet. New Mexico's San Juan, Colorado's South Platte, or the spring creeks of Montana's Paradise Valley are just a few of these delightful waters. On the other hand, more than six casts in each tiny pool in a small mountain stream with a sparse food supply and spooky trout are probably a waste of time. Small stream trout usually grab anything that looks remotely edible. If they don't eat, you've spooked them or the pool is empty, so you can move on. When fishing a small stream, it's not unusual to cover a half mile of water in an hour.

Most streams will fall in between these extremes. How fast you move should depend on what kind of fly you are using, whether you see trout feeding or not, and whether you feel like moving or not. There are no right or wrong answers. When fishing a streamer fly you should move all the time, never throwing more than two casts to the same spot. If a trout doesn't grab a streamer on the first pass it will ignore subsequent casts, no matter how hard you flog the water. If you are fishing a dry fly "blind" (that is, not fishing to visibly rising fish), more than a dozen casts in the same foot-square spot are a waste. If you see trout rising to insects, you can stay in one spot, changing flies, tippet sizes, and casting angles until you catch them or spook them. This summer I fished for a single large brown trout on the River Test in England for more than an hour, gave up, came back an hour later, and finally hooked the fish after another hour of changing flies and casting angles.

The other instance where moving is not necessary is when you are fishing a nymph, you are sure the trout are feeding, and you are sure there are many fish in front of you. This often happens in clear spring creeks or tailwaters where you can see trout feeding under the surface. Trout in these clear, rich streams may ignore your nymph for 200 casts because something was not quite right with the drift, then inhale the fly on cast number 201.

If you don't see fish under the water or feeding on the surface, you have to guess how long you should spend in one spot. A typical time for fishing a pool 50 feet wide by 100 feet long might be a half hour. In this time you'd try to hit all the likely spots you are going to learn about in a few pages. You might change flies three or four times. If you haven't caught a fish or had a strike in 30 minutes, it's probably time to move on. Perhaps someone was in this pool earlier and spooked the trout, or maybe more trout are feeding a few pools upstream.

In small mountain streams, you should approach each pool cautiously but not waste much time in each place.

4

MIDSTREAM ROCKS

READING THE WATER IS THE SKILL OF predicting where trout will lie in a stream. It's not an art, and it's not intuitive, but it requires some common sense, knowledge of what a trout needs, and an understanding of some basic hydraulics. Unless you see fish in the water, reading a stream is all guesswork. By using the following two principles, you'll be able to gain a basic understanding of any new water:

Trout find a comfortable spot where hydraulics let them feed from the current without expending too much energy.

• Trout need relatively slow water when lying in wait for prey, but prefer to be on the edge of fast water so they receive a constant supply of food from the current.

• Current in a stream is slowed by friction close to the bottom, along the banks, and in front of and behind objects.

Most stream trout are drift feeders, which means they lie in one place and let the current bring food to them. A trout may not range more than ten feet all season long, unless it is frightened and has to evade a predator. A trout finds a spot (or a series of them) in a pool or run where it can lie in almost zero velocity current yet tip up into the flow when it spies a piece of drifting food. It may rotate from one spot to another, but each spot will be a discrete place on the bottom where the hydraulics are just right. In a large pool, some trout (mostly fish over 16 inches) will move from the depths into shallow water in the early morning and evening, moving hundreds of feet for a brief hour of shallow-water feeding.

Trout prefer shallow water because it contains all the food. Insects, minnows, and stuff that falls into the water from land, such as grasshoppers and ants, are all more abundant in shallow water. A few trout in each population become cannibals and rely mostly on ambushing smaller fish like minnows or even young trout, or prey like crayfish. These trout are the ones that live in deep dark pools, feeding mostly under the cover of darkness. The problem is that they don't feed as often as drift feeders, nor are there as many of them in a stream as drift feeders. Consequently, most of your fishing should be done in shallow water.

What do I mean by shallow? Trout seem to prefer water between one foot and four feet deep. Any deeper and they don't find much food; any shallower and they feel exposed to predators. Trout do need some depth nearby, as they will bolt for the security of deep water when frightened. Wading a stream, you'll often see trout holding in the bottom of a deep pool. You may not realize you spooked the fish, and that they were rising in the shallow water at the tail of the pool five minutes before.

In a river where most of the water is deep (more than four feet) you'll find most of the fish in the shallowest water, where it's easier for them to feed. In streams where most of the water is shallow (less than a foot deep), you'll

Trout will typically be found in these spots around a midstream rock.

find most of the fish in the deeper water, where they feel secure.

The prototypical stream-reading example is a rock in the middle of the current. It's obvious at this point that trout will lie in the slack water behind the rock. Less apparent are the spots at the edges and in front of the rock, and the plume of slower current that extends quite a distance behind it. The size of the rock and the current speed determine where trout might be found.

Trout will usually be found immediately behind a grapefruit-sized rock. As rocks get bigger, the slack water behind the rock becomes almost stagnant and devoid of food because it does not get refreshed with current slipping around its sides. With a rock the size of a car, trout will thus be found farther downstream, where currents slipping around either side of the rock come together in a V shape, facing downstream.

The place immediately behind a rock may also be devoid of trout if the current is too fast. Water rushing over a rock forms turbulence, where the current rushes in all directions at once. When this turbulence becomes so harsh that water swirls like a maelstrom, trout have trouble holding their position. It's also difficult for them to feed here, because they can't predict from what angle their prey might approach.

Trout can be found in front of as well as behind a rock the size of a bowling ball. Current slamming into the front of the rock slows down, and this area of low velocity piles up in front of the rock and forms a cushion of slack water. You'll be able to spot this by the slight hump of water in front of the rock. The current may also dig a small trench in front of the rock, a perfect place for a trout to lie in wait for food—in fact the best spot in some cases, because trout can see what's coming. The same can happen along the sides of a rock, especially if a trench has formed there as well.

There is a difference between rocks that are fully submerged and rocks that stick above the surface. Even without polarized glasses, or when the water is not clear, you can find most submerged rocks by looking for humps in the surface. The bigger the hump, the bigger the rock. When a rock is fully submerged, food carried by the current slips over the top, so the area immediately behind it is a fine place for a trout to feed. Once the water level drops and the rock sticks above the water, pushing all of the food to each side, trout will move to either side or to a place farther behind the rock, so they can pluck items from the drift.

You'll often find jumbles of rocks together on the bottom. Here you read the water by trying to figure out where most of the current is channeled, then look for trout in the edges of slower water next to this flow. Suppose you find three basketball-sized rocks in the middle of some fast water, with the rocks arranged in a triangle, with the point facing upstream. The most likely place for a trout would be just in front of the two lower rocks on either side, where the fish can enjoy the cushion of water below the upper rock and in front of the lower rock—yet still have access to the main part of the current for feeding.

The drop in elevation can determine where a trout can live. In fact, given a piece of river where the slope is steep and the water runs quickly, you will find far more trout in a stretch of pocket water than one where the surface is smooth but fast. Smooth water tells you there are few obstructions on the bottom, which means there are few places where trout can live.

FISHING POCKET WATER AND MID-STREAM ROCKS

The best place to start fishing around a midstream rock is where the current slips around its sides. Here, the current is uniform and drag presents few problems. In contrast, the slack water directly behind the rock swirls in all directions, and no matter what kind of fly you pitch here, it

Pocket water gives you lots of options—trout can be anywhere.

will soon be wrenched in an unnatural direction by the conflicting currents. My approach is to first cast into the easy water, hoping that any trout in the swirls will see the fly and dart out to grab it. This works better with smaller rocks: As the area behind the rock gets larger, a trout is less likely to see your fly.

Depending on water conditions and the presence of insects, you'll want to start with either a dry or a nymph. It's an easy cast, and seldom will you need to throw any slack or fancy curves. If the rock is small, cast about a foot above it and to one side, letting your dry or nymph slip down through the seam along the rock's edge. Once you are satisfied that you've covered the edges properly, move back to the point where the current tongues along the sides of the rock converge. Don't try to fish the water just behind the rock and this piece at the same time—you'll need some special tricks for the water just behind the rock. Because the current here often pushes back toward the surface, you'll need to throw some slack into your dry-fly presentation to counteract drag. When fishing a nymph, you'll need to add some weight to your leader or drive the nymph into the water with a tuck cast. You make a tuck cast by completing the forward cast with a high, quick snap of the wrist that pushes the tip of the rod below the horizontal, instead of finishing the cast with the rod tip parallel to the water. The tuck cast drives your nymph into the water and creates a pile of slack in your leader right on top of the fly, so the fly has a chance to sink before the leader snatches it back to the surface.

Now you're ready for the water just behind the rock. It's not as productive as other places around a rock, but if you want to fish thoroughly, give it a try. If you're using a dry fly, you'll find this place difficult to fish from directly below, because the water under the tip of your rod is always faster than the water just behind the rock, and drag will often set in immediately, before a trout has had a chance to notice your fly. I like to move upstream, even with the spot behind the rock, and throw lots of slack into my leader (or add a longer tippet for a cushion against drag), and keep the rod tip high as the fly drifts. In other words, keep as much line off the water as possible. Another option is to throw an upstream curve or mend into your line so that most of the line and leader fall above the rock, or even on top of it.

When fishing a nymph in the slick behind a rock, a strike indicator is helpful—almost essential if you don't already have one attached to your leader. Even with a strike indicator, resign yourself to the fact that you will have trouble figuring out where your nymph is drifting and that strikes will be soft and difficult to detect. If the rock is submerged, cast your fly so it lands either right over the rock or even a bit upstream, if the current is fast or the water deep. If the rock is above the water, try slamming your nymph into the water right behind it with a tuck cast, or cast even with the rock on either side, hoping the current will steer your nymph into the water behind it.

Now you are ready for the pocket in front of the rock. There are a number of reasons to leave this piece for last. First, since you will be moving upstream to try to keep yourself in a trout's blind spot, it makes sense in your approach. Second, if the rock is large, you can't see in front of it and won't be able to see any strikes. And third, because you will be drifting your fly into the face of the rock, you may hang up; and if you have to wade over to retrieve your fly, it's nice to know you have at least fished all of the water behind the rock before disturbing the water. You may choose to place yourself behind and at an angle to the rock, even with it, or above it if the water is fast and deep enough so that you won't spook the trout.

Whether you choose a dry or nymph, make sure your fly drifts right up against the rock on some of your casts. Trout in a trench in front of a submerged rock often can't see a fly drifting a foot to either side, or may not be inclined to leave their haven unless food drifts right into them.

Dry flies and nymphs are natural choices for fishing midstream rocks, but you can also have fun using a streamer, wet fly, or unweighted nymph. These offerings can be effective when the currents are so swirling and conflicting that a drag-free drift is impossible. You'll be moving downstream instead of upstream, so you'll want to hit the pocket in front of the rock first. A streamer should be cast so that it sinks and drifts until right in front of the rock, and then is stripped out of the pocket like a baitfish trying to escape. Your wet fly or nymph should be cast so that it rises and swings right in front of the rock. This means casting your fly well ahead of the rock and to the far side, and planning the drift of the fly like a chess move.

You can fish the water behind a rock with a wet fly, carefully swinging the fly into all the potential hot spots. A trout will move a long way for a streamer and will usually hit it on the first drift or not at all. Thus you can fish quickly with a streamer by casting it just behind the rock and to the far side, stripping as soon as it hits the water. The streamer will often swim through all the hot spots in one cast, and drag will not be an issue because you are providing all the action.

Pocket water is just a whole mess of submerged rocks. It's often difficult to wade in pocket water, because every time you plant your foot it slips off the edge of a slippery boulder or rock. Don't try to fish every rock in a piece of pocket water—you'll exhaust yourself physically and mentally. Instead, look for rocks or groups of rocks that have a good combination of current depth and flow. Search for places where the main current threads its way through in low water, or for sheltered places along the edge in fast water. Whatever you do, don't ignore rocks right along the bank in pocket water. Our natural inclination is to look out to the middle of a piece of pocket water, but most of the fish will often be within a few feet of the bank.

This angler discovered the deep trench in front of a midstream rock—the hard way!

5

THE HEAD OF A POOL

POOLS ARE PLACES WHERE A RIVER widens and deepens for various reasons—a depression in the streambed, a collection of rocks damming the flow, or a sharp bend where water is slowed by friction with the banks. Pools can be as small as a bathtub or as large as several football fields, and can contain trout of all sizes. They usually harbor the biggest trout in a river. They are also the most heavily fished places in a given river.

Pools change character with the seasons. In spring, when the water is typically fast and high, the middle of a pool may be too fast for a trout to lie comfortably waiting for prey. Fish will be found where the current is slowest—near the banks, at the tail, and at the head, if there are rocks or a lip over which the current flows. As the season progresses and the water level falls and the current lessens, lies along the edges will become too shallow and may even dry up. The current may also become stagnant along the edges, so it won't bring trout food quickly enough. During lower flows, the best way to find trout in a pool is to look for the bubble or drift line. This is a thread of bubbles and debris that traces a path through the pool. Sometimes the drift line will break up into several threads; other times it will be a single line snaking its way from head to tail. Feeding trout will be found right under this drift line, because it is loaded with food.

Pools are typically divided into a head, middle, and tail. The current is nearly always quickest at the head, slower in the middle, and faster again at the tail. Heads of pools often have wonderful trout habitat and the water is pretty easy to read. It's also the easiest place to catch fish, because the

Fishing the "eye" at the head of a pool.

fast, turbulent current hides your approach, casting mistakes, and the fraudulent nature of your fly. Both sides of the head of a pool have areas of slick water called eyes, where friction with the bank slows the current. The current adjacent to the eyes is often the best place in a pool to pitch your fly. Another great place is where the rushing water at the head of a pool starts to slow down. You can find this spot by looking where the surface of the water starts to flatten

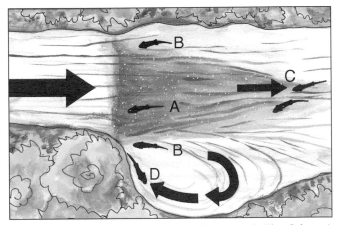

Places to look for trout at the head of a pool. The fish at A is just below the shelf where the pool deepens. The trout at B are in the seam between fast and slow water. The fish at C are in the place where the fast water begins to slow, and the trout at D is in the whirlpool, facing downstream but upcurrent.

and is merely dimpled with turbulence rather than tossed in all directions. There is often a shelf in this spot that quickly drops into deeper water. The water below this shelf is sheltered from the current, slow enough to allow a trout to lie there, waiting for food to drift overhead.

A bend in a river will often form a pool. Note that a bend always has an outside, where the water is quicker and deeper; and an inside, where the water is slower and shallower. Where most trout will be found depends on the depth and speed of the current. In a shallow stream, with average depths of less than two feet, most trout will be found on the outside of the bend, where the water is deep enough to offer them security. In deeper rivers trout may be found on the inside *and* the outside of the bend. Few trout may be found where current in a bend is fast enough to form standing waves as it hits the bank on the outside, because they can't feed and hold their position in the swift flow. The only time you'll find many trout here is if there is an obstruction like a boulder or log on the outside of the bend to break the current. Otherwise, trout will be found feeding on the slower, more comfortable current on the inside.

Fishermen sometimes get lured into casting toward the juicier-looking outside and wade right in, ignoring the inside of the bend. If you do, you might overlook the

This seam at the inside of a fast bend in the river should be the prime spot.

best fishing in the pool. The inside typically has a gradually sloping shelf that deepens downstream and toward the center of the river. Trout lie comfortably on this shelf, dining on insects washed into the pool from the riffle above. Trout will move up into shallower water during heavy insect hatches. On the South Fork of the Snake in Idaho, I have seen big cutthroats packed into the inside of a bend like sardines with their backs out of the water. Fish on the shallow inside will be spooky, though, so approach them from downstream and with great care.

HOW TO FISH THE HEAD OF A POOL

The head is the easiest part of a pool to fish. If the pool is longer than a railroad car, I like to start fishing it at the head, especially if I am not familiar with the water. The fast current here hides your approach and mistakes in your presentation, and trout lying in the head often have to grab their prey instantly, without the luxury of inspecting a fly they might have in slower currents. Enter a pool just below where the current flattens into goosebump-like riffles. Look for rising fish first; if you see risers, start with them in the downstream end and along the near edge first, work-

Fishing that magic place where the fast water at the head of a pool begins to flatten.

ing right up to the foamy water at the extreme head of the pool last. If you see trout rising in the flat water below but none in the head, thoroughly fish all of the fast water at the head anyway. You often won't be able to see trout rising in the white water but they will be, especially along the edges of the fastest water. Be extremely careful with trout rising along the eyes at either side of the head. Not only will drag be tricky here, but there may be whirlpools and trout may be facing you. Casting to these fish requires a careful approach and a presentation that puts slack into your line and leader, so your fly will drift without a hint of drag.

Most insects hatch in riffles. If there is a hatch, many of the insects that trout see will not be fully emerged. Mayflies may be half in and half out of their nymph shucks and caddisflies may be in their pupal form right at the surface. If you see insects on the water or in the air, start with an emerger instead of a high-floating dry fly. Egg-laying mayfly spinners and caddisflies usually form dense flights and fall over riffles as well, so the riffle at the head of a pool will be the first place you notice fish rising. If the humidity is low and hatching insects are leaving the water quickly, sometimes the head of a pool is the only place you'll see fish rising, because most of the bugs will get airborne before they get to the slow water in the middle of a pool.

If no trout are rising and if the water is fast or deep, the best method is to fish a nymph with a strike indicator. Start at the near edge of the place where the current begins to flatten, move to the middle, and then fish the far edge. When fishing the far edge, raise your rod tip to keep most of the fly line above the current in the middle; otherwise the faster, closer flow will snatch your line and leader, putting instant drag into your drift. Gradually move toward the head of the pool. Look for the place where the bottom drops off—it will show up as darker water and trout will lie here waiting for food drifting over the edge. When you get to the foamy water at the head, fish even more thoroughly. Trout here will not be able to see your fly as well and it might take a dozen drifts in the same area to put the nymph close enough to a feeding fish. About the only way to get your nymph under the faster current at the surface and into the quieter water below, and to maintain a dead drift at the same time, is to cast into the shallow water above the head of the pool. This will let your nymph tumble into the pool in a way that looks natural to the fish.

It's helpful to use a tuck cast at the eyes on either side of the head, because the surface current here is usually much faster than the current just below. If you don't drive your nymph below the surface, it will be pulled back up by your leader and indicator. As in most places with complicated currents, strikes here may be tough to detect and you should strike at the subtlest dip of your indicator.

Streamers work great in the head of a pool, especially if the water is cold or high and there is no insect activity. Contrary to the way streamers are usually fished at the head of a pool—by standing at the top, firing the fly across the head and then stripping back against the current—I like to fish a streamer upstream in this situation. This gives my fly a chance to sink and tumble in the current before I start yanking on it. To do it, stand well below the head of the pool and cast your streamer into the tumbling water in the center. If your streamer is not weighted and the pool is more than two feet deep, add some weights such as sink putty or tin shot about six inches above the fly. Give your fly a few seconds to tumble in the current or even throw a slack mend into the line by flipping some line over the top of the leader with an abbreviated roll cast. Then begin stripping the streamer back toward you. It will rise from the depths, often provoking a strike from trout that have ignored nymphs and dry flies.

6

THE MIDDLE OF A POOL

THE MIDDLE OF A POOL CAN AT FIRST appear to be featureless. The water is often flat, with a uniform speed and no bulges that indicate rocks on the bottom. Look for some kind of features on the bottom—rocks, logs, or patches of weed—if the water is clear enough. Any roughening of the bottom will harbor trout; they avoid flat, featureless bottoms of sand, mud, or bedrock. Next, investigate the depth: Look for water that is two to three feet deep. If most of the pool is six feet deep, look for the shallow stuff; if most of the pool is ankle-deep, look for depressions on the bottom where the water is a little deeper.

Perhaps the most productive spot for finding trout in a pool is along a deep bank. Here trout can have the security of deep water close by, yet they can slide onto the lip along the bank and feed on floating insects. The current along the bank is slowed by friction, yet there is easy access to the food carried by the current. Banks also offer subterranean refuge in the little caves where the current cuts under the bank. The prime spot along a deep bank is where a little point of land or a large rock sticks out, forming a sheltered bay.

Rough, rocky banks hold more trout than smooth banks. Trees that have fallen into the water, called sweepers, offer both protection and shelter from the current. Trout will normally be found feeding in front of sweepers and right at their tips and not in the stagnant, food-poor water behind the trunk.

The middle of a pool can be especially productive if the water is deep enough to hold trout and there is a break from the current. Midstream rocks, currents that converge (called seams), fallen logs, or abrupt changes in depth all produce that all-important edge between water slow enough for trout to rest and current fast enough to bring them food.

When trout in a slow pool realize there is a large amount of food on the water, but that it is not getting to them fast enough, they'll start to cruise. I've watched a large trout eat a mayfly, look around, wait for another one, and then start to swim upstream or to the side, as if impatient with the amount of food coming to it. Typically, a trout will cruise upstream, rising at regular intervals, until it reaches the head of a pool or the water gets too fast or

The middle of this pool has it all—a big rock against the far bank, large cobbles on the bottom, and a deep slot in the middle.

shallow. Then it will turn around and swim downstream to repeat the process, usually not feeding on the return trip. You'll see this in slow pools, and the trout that do it will be bigger than average.

HOW TO FISH THE MIDDLE OF A POOL

The middle of a pool is usually where you'll see trout rising, so it's important to study the water for rises before you jump in and start flailing away. There may be fish rising where you were going to step into the pool; if so, back up and walk downstream until you can get into the river below them. The best approach to avoid spooking fish is always directly below them. You are in their blind spot, and because you are standing in the same current as your quarry, drag is easier to avoid. As long as you cast only the tippet of your leader over a rising trout, you'll seldom spook one; it's when the heavier and more opaque fly line drops on top of them that fish become frightened enough to stop feeding.

I'm assuming you have chosen the shallow side of a pool for wading. If trout are rising in the middle of a pool or along the far bank, and you are able to wade directly below them, you will be able to catch them more easily. The water here is often too deep to wade, however, so

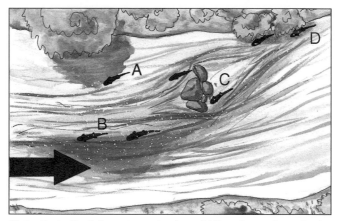

Note that all of these trout in the middle of a pool are in the bubble that carries the bulk of insects and debris through a pool. The fish at A is in the shade of a willow tree. The two trout at B are on the edge of a deep channel. The pair of fish at C are near a jumble of midstream rocks. The two at D are just below tiny points of land jutting off a deep bank.

you have to use an upstream-and-across, directly across, or downstream-and-across presentation. There are advantages to these angles, because only the fly and a small segment of the tippet will pass over a trout's head. Also, trout feeding against the far bank are invariably in water that is slower than the water out in the middle, where your line and most of your leader will fall. If you cast a fly to these trout, the faster current will snatch the line and cause the fly to drag. By getting upstream of these fish and casting at a downstream angle, you'll buy yourself a little time against unnatural movement. Throwing some slack and upstream curves will amplify your drag protection.

Most insects hatch in the faster water at the head of a pool, so you will see fully emerged insects more often in the middle. However, many insects take a long time to break free of their shucks, drifting just under the surface before hatching, so don't rule out seeing emergers in the middle of a pool, either. In addition to mayflies and caddisflies, you'll see midges hatching in the middle more often

Angler Walt Wetherell is working along the bank of this big river, searching for rising fish.

than the head, so be ready to go to tiny flies if you see trout sipping. Another scenario that can fool you is a flight of mayfly spinners or egg-laying caddis. In a long pool, insects can be falling in the riffles a hundred yards away, but you won't see anything in the middle of the pool. Trout rising to spent insects flush in the surface film will be nearly invisible unless you get your face close to the surface or check the surface film with an aquarium net.

If trout in the middle of a pool aren't rising you can sometimes take them on a dry anyway. If the weather is warm and terrestrial insects are active, an ant, beetle, or grasshopper fly can draw strikes, especially if you can fish it over the deep water along the far bank. The slower the current, however, the less likely a dry fly will work unless you see at least a couple of rising fish.

If a pool is not too large, or if you know the stream you are fishing has a high density of trout, a nymph might be your fly of choice if nothing is rising. If you can pick out features such as submerged rocks, or changes between fast and slow or shallow and deep, an upstream presentation might be a smart move, because it is easier to make your fly appear natural when it is fished upstream without drag. But unless you want to drive yourself crazy, stick to the places that look fishy. Fishing a nymph upstream requires the most concentration of any type of fishing, and trying to cover a featureless pool the size of a city block can seem futile. Because midpool trout won't grab a fly with the same abandon they will in faster water, and because the current is not moving as fast, strikes to a nymph will be more subtle here. You'll definitely miss some of the strikes without an indicator.

When working a big pool, it's often more relaxing to fish a nymph or wet fly across-and-downstream, because you can cover more water with less effort. Take your indicator off and remove any weight on the leader, as these seem to hinder the effectiveness of a fly swinging in the current. You should cast at a slight upstream angle with a little slack if the water is deep, following the fly's progress with your rod tip. The sight of your fly rising to the surface as the line tightens can often stimulate a trout into grabbing it before it escapes. Flies with some soft hackle or other flowing material seem to work better, as opposed to the hard-bodied patterns you might choose to fish in the faster water at the head of the pool. I've also found that smaller patterns work better in slow water—if a Size 14 fly is working in fast riffles or at the head of a pool, switch to a Size 16 or 18 in the middle.

The middle of a pool screams for a streamer if there is absolutely no insect activity and you don't have any idea where the trout are. One cast to each likely spot is enough, and if the pool is not too wide, you can work through even a big pool in short order. You'll get best results by wading into the middle of the river and casting directly across the current to the deep bank, stripping line constantly all the way back to your rod tip. If the water is very deep, throw a couple of upstream mends into your drift as soon as the fly hits the water so you can get it down to the trout. A weighted fly and/or a sink-tip line can also help. Many times trout will chase your streamer but won't take it. These fish usually won't take any fly right after they've chased a streamer. You at least know where they live, though, and might even be able to predict where trout are in the rest of the pool by studying the places they've come from.

7

THE TAIL OF A POOL

THE TAIL OF A POOL IS THE MOST MISUN-
derstood, difficult to fish, and underfished place in most
trout streams. However, with the right techniques and
some observation, it can be the most productive place in
a river, particularly for larger fish. As water runs from the
middle of a pool into the tail, the stream channel often gets
narrower and nearly always gets shallower. Food carried by
the current is concentrated vertically and horizontally, so a
trout lying in the tail sees more food drift by than a trout
in any other place in the pool.

The shallows at the tail are often filled with other prey,
such as minnows and crayfish—the stuff that grows big
trout. And bigger trout prefer to live in places where they
can see the approach of predators, as the need to stay on
guard seems to be as important as the need to be hidden.
Pools that have boulder-studded tails are more productive

than a smooth gravel bottom because there are more places for trout to hide and more slack water refuges to get out of the current.

You'll often see a deep slot along one or both banks right at the downstream end of a tail. These spots can be deceptively deep and are choice lies for big fish. Add a big rock or two along the bank and some overhanging brush and you might just have the best spot in the entire pool for a large trout. These fish are sometimes impossible to approach unless they are heavily preoccupied with a hatch.

I have a favorite pool on the big Delaware River on the border between New York and Pennsylvania that consistently produces huge trout for me. The head of the pool below and the head of the pool above my spot are often full of anglers during the evening hatch, yet my spot is often empty (unusual on this heavily fished river). I hardly ever see trout here during the day, and even at the beginning of the evening hatch few fish will be rising. Yet once the sun drops below the surrounding hills and the water is covered with insects, trout appear almost magically. Most are well over average size. I am not sure whether they move down into the tail from the huge deep pool above, or whether they live in the deep slots alongside the rocks in the tail itself. I do know that by dark it looks like a convention of every big boy in the Delaware.

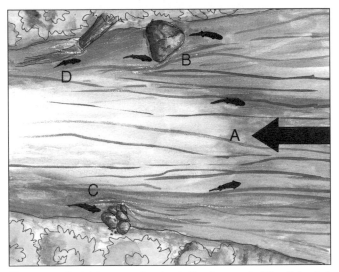

Places to find big trout in the tail of a pool. The fish at A are at the point where deep water from the pool hits the shallow bar at the beginning of the tail. The trout at B and C are lying along rocks set into the bank. The fish at D is lying alongside a submerged log.

HOW TO FISH THE TAIL OF A POOL

The tail of a pool conspires against you at every step. The water is shallower than in the rest of the pool, so trout are always on the alert because they don't have the security of deeper water over their heads. (Even though a trout in shallow water sees less of the outside world than one in deep water, trout in deep water won't always feel threatened by your approach because they feel secure.) The water at the tail is invariably smooth, and trout can see you through a smooth surface much easier than they can through a broken surface.

Compounding this is a piece of water that is always faster at its downstream end, where it picks up speed as the bottom becomes shallower. When you try to approach trout from their downstream blind spot in the tail, every cast drags almost instantly, because the faster water under your rod tip yanks the fly back toward you. It's easier to

The tail of a pool is one of the best places to find trout, and one of the hardest to fish.

present a fly downstream in the tail of a pool because the water at your feet is slower than the water you're fishing over. However, by doing this you approach trout from upstream and risk spooking them!

I'd advise you to approach trout rising in the tail of a pool in a crouch or by kneeling in the shallow water. If you can sneak up one side or the other, your profile will be hidden against streamside brush. Watch the fish—between the spookiness of the fish and the knowledge that half of your casts will drag as soon as they hit the water (unless you are a far better caster than most), you must make every cast count. One cast that will help in this case is the parachute cast, in which you aim your forward cast high in the air, at about 11 o'clock, so that the leader and line fall to the surface in big coils. Practice this cast before you use it over rising fish to make sure you can be accurate with it. Adding a long tippet—at least 3 feet long and preferably 6—will also help you avoid drag in this tricky position.

Sometimes you can approach trout rising in the tail from above, most often if the river is wide enough so you can stay off to the side a bit, or after the sun has left the water and the fish have become bolder. Use the parachute cast here, again, or throw an upstream curve cast to keep the fly from dragging before it passes over the fish.

After hatches or spinner falls, fish in the tail may con-
tinue to rise long after those in the upper part of the pool
have stopped. These fish take advantage of the funneling
effect of the tail, catching all the spent or crippled insects
that have washed through the pool. By moving to the tail
after the hatch is over, you can often extend your dry-fly
fishing an hour or more.

I find fishing the tail especially difficult with a dry fly
if there is no hatch. If you don't know exactly where trout
may be lying, blind casting over them usually frightens
more fish than it attracts, because you can't tell when you

Even in a huge river like New York's Delaware, tails of
pools require a cautious approach.

are dropping your line right on top of them. Drag-free drifts are so short that it's difficult to get a rise unless you have a precise target. One way of getting fish to rise in the tail of a pool is by skating a caddis. This seldom works unless caddisflies have been hatching in the last day or two. Attach a heavily hackled caddis imitation to a greased leader (coat the entire leader with paste dry-fly dressing or line dressing), approach from upstream, and cast across and downstream, about three feet above a place you think a trout may be lying. As soon as the fly hits the water, raise your rod tip almost to a vertical position and, wiggling the rod tip from side to side, bring your rod tip back over your shoulder and strip some line so the fly skates across the surface. Then drop your rod tip abruptly so the fly drifts downstream, drag-free on the slack you've created. Strikes will be vicious and it's exciting fishing. This technique only works in smooth, fast current, which is why it is most often used in the tail of a pool.

Like dry-fly fishing, nymph fishing in the tail is difficult without a target. However, because the water in the tail is often shallow and clear, it's possible to sight-fish trout with a small weighted nymph. Watch for fish weaving in the current. The ones that dart from side to side are feeding on aquatic insects and can be caught, provided you don't spook them with your presentation. Take strike indicators and any weight off your leader and cast about a foot to one side of the trout, leading the fish enough so that your fly sinks. Be careful to drop only the leader and not the line on top of the fish. When you see the trout dart to one side at the point where you think your fly is just even with the fish, tighten gently on the line. Don't strike too hard. If the fish was not taking your fly, gently tightening won't disturb the water and may get another chance. By all means, if you see a trout moving its head like a dog shaking a rubber toy, strike! It has probably taken your fly and is trying to dislodge it.

Streamers seem to work better in the tails of pools than any other place. I'm not sure if it's because there are often more baitfish in the tail, more big fish, or the current there is just right for presenting a streamer. I do know that I will often go through an entire pool without a strike, only to finally connect when I throw my fly into the tail. The best approach is to cast to the far bank and strip the fly across the current with a brisk motion. Don't worry about getting your fly down here; the water in the tail is shallow enough so that fish always see your streamer. If a trout is interested, it will smash it!

8

RIFFLES AND RUNS

DON'T JUST HAUNT CLEARLY DEFINED pools. Riffles and runs—areas of fast water with no distinct heads and tails—can often be extremely productive places to fish. Typically, they aren't fished as heavily as pools, and because the water is moving swiftly with a broken surface, it's easier to fool trout with imitations. The term riffle is used to describe a piece of relatively shallow water, usually without big rocks or other big obstructions on the bottom. Runs are typically narrower and deeper, but the terms are often used interchangeably. Some rivers are composed almost entirely of riffles and runs, with few distinct pools.

Much of this water is too fast or too shallow to hold trout over six inches long, so the challenge here is to locate the deeper, slower pieces of water. I find it helpful to step back some distance from a riffle and look at the whole picture. Good holding water is a relative term, and what might be prime stuff in one riffle could be marginal in another. Let's say you are looking at one long riffle, 100 yards long, 50 yards wide, and at first glance all the same depth. You can actually see the slope of a riffle, tilting down from the upstream to downstream end like a big cookie sheet. If you look carefully, though, you'll see dents in the cookie sheet: There are little pockets throughout any riffle where the water slows and deepens. Here is where you should fish.

Once you get an idea of where the pockets are, look for other features. The obvious place is where a riffle begins

You can see the slick places just above and below this angler, indicating the deeper, slower places in this riffle.

to tumble, and just as there is at the head of a pool, there should be a deeper slot here where the current's force has cut into the streambed. You should also look for flat spots or "slicks" in the riffle. These are places where the riffle is either slower or deeper; they often hold trout. If you can't see any slicks and most of the bottom of the riffle is visible through your polarized glasses, search for places where you can't see bottom. Any spot in a riffle that is just a little deeper than the rest will provide trout with security and protection from the current. In streams with abundant food and a dense trout population, even a slot the size of a desktop can hold fish. In streams with average productivity, look for places at least as big as a large dining room table.

In runs and deeper, faster riffles, the most important features to look for are seams. These are clearly defined places where fast water meets slow, which creates turbulence and a reduction of the overall energy of the current. A seam is a great place for trout to lie; here they can rest in the slower water but dart quickly into the food-carrying current. If the current in the middle of the river is slow to moderate (up to the speed of a fast walk), more trout will be found in the seam than in the middle of the river. If the current is any faster than a walk, and without midstream objects, the seams (and the slower water along the bank, if it is more than two feet deep) may be the only places you'll find fish.

A well-defined seam at the edge of a riffle. Trout will be concentrated along this line.

HOW TO FISH RIFFLES AND RUNS

I love to fish riffles. They are often overlooked by anglers, so trout there may not see as many flies during a season, they are unlikely to be spooked on any given day. A bonus is that the fast, broken water hides your mistakes in your presentation. On a trip to the Provo River near Park City, Utah, I was having trouble getting strikes in the better-looking pools. The Provo has an abundant brown trout population and I knew I was placing my fly over several fish on each cast. I noticed most other anglers were ignoring the riffles, so I decided to work my small midge nymph in a riffle that at first glance looked too slow and shallow.

Careful observation of a riffle on the Bighorn showed this fish rising while making little disturbance.

Jim Logan delivered a tiny midge pattern to that subtle rise and took this nice brown.

When I started wading the riffle, however, I found slightly deeper and slower spots along the bank, under streamside brush. Each one of these little pockets yielded a trout about 16 inches long—and in the deepest pocket, no bigger than a large bathtub, I hooked five nice trout.

The best part of fishing in riffles is that I could have caught those fish on a dry or a streamer as well as a nymph. Trout lying in riffles are typically in shallow water, and, being closer to the surface, they can see every fly that goes over them, whether it's in the surface film or under water. They also don't get as good a look at a fly as in a pool, so they must either grab the fly without hesitation or go hungry.

The most important part of fishing riffles is actually finding the fish. If you can find trout in a riffle, and the water is clear and the temperature is between 55 and 70°F, any fly that is recognized as a familiar food should take them. The same can't be said about pools, where even a perfect drift over feeding trout may be ignored because the fish get such a good look at your fly.

The Ausable Wulff is a near-perfect attractor dry: White wings for visibility, lots of hackle for flotation, and good bulk to attract a trout's attention.

Anglers often ignore riffles during insect hatches. It's difficult to see trout rising in the broken water, but don't give up. Most insects hatch in riffles, and the opportunity to find rising trout here is greater than anyplace else in a river. Unlike fishing a pool, in a riffle you really must get

Large Bead–Head Prince Nymph

Small Pheasant–Tail nymph

A two–nymph tandem rig.

into the water and get close to a likely spot before you'll be able to spot rising fish. You can get closer to trout in riffles than in slower water because it is difficult for the fish to see above the surface, and because the waves you make when wading are instantly dissipated. Once you're in the riffle, look upstream into the slicks where the water is slightly deeper and slower. In deep slicks, you'll often see the splash of a feeding fish—which you can easily distinguish from the riffled current. In shallow slicks, particularly those along the bank, you will often see sedate rises that appear as dark snouts poking out of the water, seldom with bubbles or splashes. These are difficult to see from more than thirty feet away, but "head-hunting" for such trout in riffles is one of the most exciting ways to fish a dry fly.

If no rises appear, don't give up. Instead, tie on a highly visible, so-called "attractor" dry, such as a Parachute, Humpy, or Wulff. Attractors are flies with lots of hackle or white wings that show a buggy profile to you and the trout. They are often caricatures of insects, with exaggerated features that seem to excite the fish. Use an attractor that's not only large enough so you can see it, but big enough to entice trout that might not be actively feeding. On rivers with stoneflies or hoppers this might call for a dry fly as large as a Size 4 or 6. In a typical freestone mountain river a Size 12 or 14 might be more appropriate—something about the size of the larger caddisflies and mayflies the fish are accustomed to eating. In the thin water of late season or in spring creeks, a productive attractor dry might be as small as a Size 18. You'll have to discover a pattern and size by trial and error, barring any helpful advice from a fellow angler or previous experience on the river.

It's important that you see your attractor fly. If you can't, you may lose sight of your fly, pick up to make a cast, and

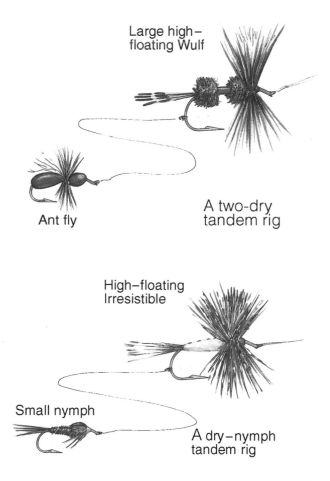

Large high–
floating Wulf

Ant fly

A two-dry
tandem rig

High–floating
Irresistible

Small nymph

A dry–nymph
tandem rig

discover a trout on the line, because trout in riffles can take your fly with barely a wrinkle in the surface. If you aren't looking right at your fly, you can miss the nose that porpoises over it.

Fishing a nymph directly upstream can be as intriguing as dry-fly fishing. In shallow riffles, you can often fish without weight on your leader or a strike indicator, which makes casting much more pleasant. Because the current is fast and the trout must grab your fly quickly, you'll see the strikes as the tip of your floating line darts upstream. One of the most productive techniques is to tie a large weighted fly onto the end of your tippet, then add a smaller, unweighted fly to a dropper tied to the bend of the hook of the larger fly.

Let's say you are fishing a stream where common nymph sizes are between Sizes 12 and 18. You've discovered this by talking to other fishermen, inquiring at a local fly shop, or turning over some rocks to see what kind of larvae the stream offers. Tie a Size 12 Bead Head Nymph, weighted Hare's Ear Nymph, or Prince Nymph to the end of a 9-foot, 5X leader. Tie an eight-inch piece of 5X or 6X tippet material to the bend of this fly with a clinch knot. Now tie a Size 18 Pheasant Tail Nymph or midge larva imitation to this lower piece.

Toss this rig into the head of a slick or along the edge of a seam. You can work a seam the size of a desktop with a dozen casts; bigger slicks will require more effort. Typically, nymphs fished like this are only effective for a short part of the drift, about halfway between your rod tip and where your flies landed. In the first part of the drift the flies have not gotten deep enough, and toward the end of the drift drag takes over and pulls your flies back to the surface. Use a tuck cast at the beginning and holding your rod tip high, and you can extend the productive part of the drift. Trout can see a dry fly from further away and usually take it on the first or second cast in the right spot. However, it might take over a dozen casts in the same place with a nymph. Maybe trout don't see it, maybe they get a better look at a nymph once they do notice it, or perhaps presentation with a nymph needs to be more precise than with a dry fly. I do know that it pays to be more thorough when fishing a nymph, particularly when the water is cold and trout aren't very aggressive.

The direct upstream approach is best in shallow riffles. In deeper seams and pockets, you'll get a better drift by fishing upstream and across; unfortunately, the most productive technique is one that is not much fun to cast—at least one heavily weighted fly or weight on the leader, plus a strike indicator. Lob this rig on a short line (less than 30 feet) upstream about 45 degrees and five feet from where you suspect a trout is feeding (even further in deeper

Nymphing with a high rod and an indicator. Unnatural drag on your nymph is almost eliminated with this technique.

water). Try to keep all or most of your fly line off the water; ideally, there should be a straight line between your rod tip and the strike indicator. This almost eliminates drag. To extend the productive drift as the flies drift downstream of your position, wiggle slack out of your rod tip so the indicator drifts in the same current lane, instead of swinging in toward your position.

Once you catch a fish on one of the flies, change the other to a pattern closer to the one that's working—or, if occasional tangles bother you, just fish with the one productive pattern.

To help detect strikes and double your odds in riffled water, you can also fish two dries at once, or a dry and a nymph combined. Commonly, a bushy fly such as a Wulff pattern is tied to the tippet and a small, less-visible fly such as an ant, beetle, or midge is used as the lower fly. The idea here is that you think the fish would eat a small fly in the riffle but you realize you'll never be able to follow it; the larger fly becomes a strike indicator, and when you see it twitch you should strike. There's also an excellent chance that the fish may take the bigger fly! Using the same setup, you can replace the lower fly with a small nymph, thus covering the water with a dry and a nymph at the same time—again, the big dry fly acts as an indicator. Just make sure that your dry is buoyant enough to stay afloat when trailing a nymph, or that your nymph is not so heavily weighted that it pulls the dry under. Frequent use of white silicate desiccant powder on your dry will keep it floating.

Trout will take streamers in riffles, but I don't think these flies are as effective here as in pools. Trout in riffles see fewer baitfish than in the shallow parts of pools, and it's harder to get a decent presentation in riffles, because the pockets are often so small that you can't get a long enough retrieve to interest the fish. If you do try a streamer in riffles, stick to the deeper runs and begin stripping your fly as soon as it hits the water.

A swung wet fly or nymph is an effective and fun way to fish riffled water. This technique works better in shallow riffles, and does not work well with strike indicators or weight on your leader. Here, you cast across stream or upstream and across. Hold your rod about 45 degrees above the water and follow the fly's progression through the riffle with the rod tip. Try to keep a straight line between the fly and the rod by mending line either upstream or down, depending on which way the current puts a bow in the line. At the end of the swing when the fly gets below you, strip in a few feet, as sometimes trout will take the fly immediately below you.

Another way to fish a swung fly is to sink the fly at the beginning of the drift by casting some slack, making an immediate upstream mend, and then making subsequent mends as the fly gets even with your position. When the fly gets just downstream of your position, or when it gets over a place where you think a trout might be lying, stop following the fly with the rod tip, or even raise the tip slightly. This forces the sunken fly to rise to the surface like a hatching insect; sometimes, trout can't resist it.

9

EFFECTS OF RIVER CONDITIONS ON APPROACH AND PRESENTATION

FISHING TINY BROOKS AND BIG RIVERS

MOST OF WHAT I HAVE SAID SO FAR APPLIES to "average" trout streams, from 20 to 100 feet wide. In small brooks and huge rivers you might need to adjust your tactics. In small brooks, it's almost imperative that you fish directly upstream: You can't fish directly across because the stream channel is too narrow, and if you fish directly downstream, trout will be able to see your every move.

Trout in small waters are very spooky, given the shallow water and the ease with which predators can grab them.

In small streams, limiting factors to trout abundance are depth and protection. There is no secret to where you'll find them—the deepest pools and places where logs or rocks give them cover. Unless you find a particularly deep pool where water is more than three feet, most pools and pockets can be fished with a dozen casts at most. After that, you've either caught all the fish or you've spooked them, as trout in tiny brooks are seldom selective and are always looking for food. Move quickly between pools, but approach each new pool with extreme caution, keeping your profile low by crouching. Stay at least 15 feet below the tail of the pool, and observe before proceeding. Where is the best place in the pool, where depth offers security and current brings the most food?

Don't overlook the tail of a pool in a small stream. Fish here are spooky and you often won't see them, because by the time you've made a cast they have already bolted for cover. The best approach is to stay well back from the tail and throw your first few casts so that only half your leader lands in the pool. Try to throw the rest of your leader and line over rocks below the pool so that your fly does not drag instantly; if there are no convenient rocks, throw slack by making a parachute cast. You will hang up on rocks and logs at the tail of the pool. Your dilemma now is whether

As long as the water temperature is above 50°F, a dry fly, cast straight upstream, is the most deadly way to fish small streams.

to break off your fly, or sneak up to the tail and unsnag it. That depends on how good the pool looks.

Once you've covered the tail, move up a bit and make a few casts in the middle of the pool. Don't waste much time here unless there are some nice rocks or a deep slot. Most of the trout you find in bathtub-sized pools will either be in the tail or the head of the pool. Cover the head thoroughly, throwing right into the foam at the lip, and don't forget the seams at either side of the head.

The best way to fish a small stream, particularly if the water is less than two feet deep, is with a dry fly. Trout in small streams don't have far to go to rise to the surface, and you can bet they'll see your dry every time. As long as the water temperature is above 50°F, a dry fly can be as effective as a worm in the right hands. Another advantage to fishing a dry is that you can put your fly up against tight spots or tiny pockets and have it become effective instantly.

Nymphs require a bit of drift to sink, and if a trout grabs your nymph as soon as it hits the water, you may not see your floating line or strike indicator twitch. I like to reserve nymphs for deeper pools, after I've tried a few casts with a dry, or when water temperatures are below 50°F. A strike indicator helps, but you'll rarely need to add any weight to your leader. Don't forget to set your indicator at

Watch for cruising trout in giant pools.

about twice the depth of the water—which will be considerably shallower than you set an indicator in most rivers.

Small streamers, such as Sizes 10 and 12, can also work in small streams. The best place for streamers is in the larger pools, especially those at the bases of small waterfalls, where trout may be reluctant to come up for a dry, or can't see it because of the white water on the surface. Cast your streamer right up into the foam, let it sink briefly, then strip it back in steady pulls right to your feet.

Trout will be everywhere you think they should be in small brooks. But in huge rivers, 100 yards wide with pools up to a quarter-mile long, you may have trouble finding them. There is no way you can effectively fish a giant pool on Montana's Missouri or New York's Delaware without narrowing down the playing field. Giant pools are usually slow, so you need to find the places where the current is swift enough to bring a steady quantity of food, which means you should concentrate in the head and the tail. Sometimes you'll find a jumble of rocks in the middle of a pool, where the concentrated flow will hold some trout. In these large pools, the deep bank is typically more productive than the shallow one, especially if the bank is rough and broken with rocks or little bays and points.

One of the best ways to find trout in large pools is to observe them with binoculars. The slow current encourages surface feeding, and because the trout might be a long way from a riffle, most of the food they see may be crippled emergers or spent spinners. Watch for cruisers. Although trout in most waters stay in one spot when feeding, if a pool is big enough and the water is slow, they will cruise looking for food because the current does not bring it to them fast enough. It's as if they get impatient waiting for the next morsel. They'll develop a pattern when cruising, and if you watch long enough, you'll be able to predict where a trout will feed and place yourself in a position to intercept it. Trout will almost always cruise upstream, then turn around and swim back to where they started, repeating the process over and over again. I once watched a large brown trout in the Connecticut River on the Vermont–New Hampshire border cruise from the tail of a 200-yard-long pool to the head and then swim all the way back to repeat the process. At first I thought there were a number of fish in the pool, and I kept moving upstream to get into position. Then I noticed that all the fish moved their heads with a peculiar sideways motion when rising, and that there was never more than one fish feeding at one time. I tried to keep up with this single cruising trout without disturbing the water, but when I finally thought I had caught up with him at the head, I turned around and saw he was already back at the tail! Then I waited and tried to intercept him when he returned, but he refused my fly

Nick Lyons suspects there is a hidden spring entering this pool on New York's Willowemoc because of the steep rock banks on the far side.

on his second pass. I finally gave up on him after playing the game for an hour. It was fun, though.

TEMPERATURE

Water temperature affects the way you approach a stream, the time of day you should fish, and how you present a fly. Approach is simple: In cold water below 50°F, trout will be found in the deeper pools, in slow water, and will not be as spooky as when they're more active. As water

If you fish nymphs slowly and deep enough, you can take trout all winter long.

warms above 50°F, they'll become more active, will slide into shallower water to feed, and will be more alert and easier to frighten.

In water below that magic 50°F number, the best fishing will be in the middle of the day, from 11 a.m. until about 3 p.m. This is when water is warmest and both trout and insects are more active. Between 50 and 55°F, trout will be active from midmorning until the sun leaves the water. At water temperatures from 55 to 65°F, trout will be active from dawn until dusk and well into the darkness if insects are still on the water. From 65 to 70°F, water temperatures become uncomfortable but tolerable for trout, and the best fishing will be from dawn until midmorning, because the water has cooled down to a minimum overnight. It's often thought that evening fishing is best in midsummer, and although you'll see some fish feeding right at dark when insects are on the water, remember that the warmest water will be in the evening. Night fishing becomes effective in this temperature range, and streamers fished on a slow swing in the tails of shallow pools can be deadly. For some reason humid nights with a new moon seem to produce the best action after dark.

Trout will feed sparingly above 70°F, but it's not really ethical to fish for them at this time. Playing a trout in 75°F water will exhaust it, and the fish will become oxygen-starved from exertion (water this warm cannot hold much

At the height of the season, when water temperatures are perfect and flow is not too high or too low, trout can be caught almost anywhere using any method.

dissolved oxygen). Most trout caught in water at their upper range will die after being released, even if carefully revived.

When most of a river is above 70°F, you can often find cold-water refuges where trout will be active and healthy. In many streams, trout move into the headwaters and tributary streams, closer to springs, and where dense shade keeps sun off the water. Steep cliffs often have subterranean springs seeping into a river, so pools along steep banks may offer cooler water than other sections. If you listen carefully, you can sometimes hear the tinkle of spring water as it enters a river along a brushy bank, unseen by the casual angler. Carry a thermometer and search for water below 65°F.

Water temperature is important when deciding how to present a fly. In water below 50°F, you'll see few fish rising and a dry fly fished "blind" will be pretty useless. Nymphs and streamers are your smart options. Nymphs should be fished right next to the bottom, completely dead drift, in slower water. If you are not hanging your fly on the bottom once every dozen casts, you are not getting deep enough. Trout will move reluctantly for a fly, so precise casting into deeper slots is essential; if your fly is a foot too far on either side of a trout, it will probably be ignored.

During high water, you might have to stick to streamers.

Streamers should also be fished deep. Cast upstream, let the fly sink, and strip line until you feel resistance. Then let the fly drift a foot or so before stripping again. This makes your fly flutter like a wounded baitfish in the current, and since it does not appear to be going anywhere in a hurry, a trout may think it's an easy target.

In water between 50 and 55°F, trout start to warm up. They'll respond to a hatch, but fishing blind with a dry fly is still not a safe bet. Nymphs should still be fished dead drift, but trout might move up more in the water column,

During low water periods, dry-fly fishing and nymphing to visible trout make this challenging time exciting as well.

so you may not have to get your fly right on the bottom. You can pick up the pace on your streamer retrieve, too.

You'll be in hog heaven with water temperatures from 55 to 65°F. You can fish a dry fly with success even if you see no rises or insects on the water. A nymph fished dead drift is still most effective, but trout will be "on the grab" and will move several feet for the fly. They'll also respond to a wet fly or nymph that is swung in the current, especially if mayflies or caddisflies are hatching. You can fish a streamer upstream, across stream, or straight downstream. Strip like mad. Trout can capture a streamer moving faster than you can strip, and in this prime temperature range a fast strip often works best, as the trout grab the fly from reflex without getting a good look at it.

Water temperatures between 65 and 70°F will usually be found only in midsummer, after most aquatic insects have hatched. Mayfly larvae left on the streambed will be tiny ones, and terrestrial insects take up the slack because of the paucity of hatches. Presentation should be cautious, and you should use light tippets and long leaders. You may see tiny mayflies and caddisflies (Size 20 and smaller) in the morning and evening, thus small dries or nymphs will be most effective. Ant, beetle, and grasshopper flies are good choices during the day. These dries and nymphs should be fished dead drift. You'll have better luck in bubbly riffles, where the oxygen content is higher, than you will in the stagnant water of slow pools.

Streamers won't work well during the day, but sometimes are quite effective at first light. Stick to patterns on the small side—Size 8 and smaller—when the water is this warm. If you can find pocket water with lots of turbulence, you might be able to tease strikes from trout on streamers until midmorning.

Stable banks and rich vegetation tell you this is a rich stream.

WATER LEVEL AND CLARITY

You can tell when a river's water is higher than normal by looking at the banks. A river in flood has narrow banks and some of the streamside brush will be under water. At times like this it can be futile to try to fish fast water or spots in the middle. Fish out there won't rise to a dry fly, and you may not be able to get your nymph deep or slow enough to look natural. What's left? Try the water right along the banks, in the tails of pools, and at the head of shallow riffles where the current is slow and shallow enough for trout to capture insects. Trout will move into these places on high water, spots that might be dry enough to pitch a tent under normal water conditions. Another place to look for them is in side channels that might be just a trickle in low water. The velocity of the current will be greatly reduced in these channels. I've had many a fishing trip saved by poking around behind islands when the water in a river looked too high for good fishing.

High, clear water is not too bad, but high, dirty water limits your options even further. Don't give up yet. Fish that have moved into shallow water can still be caught on dry flies if the water clarity is a foot or more. Because dirty water carries a lot of debris with it, though, nymph fishing can be difficult. It seems like the fish give up trying to discern food from junk when there's too much inedible

In a rich steam, fishing to risers is smarter than trying
to blind-fish with a dry.

stuff in the flow. Sometimes a wet fly or nymph swung in slower currents will draw strikes, as the motion of the fly contrary to the current tells the fish your fly is something other than trash.

Streamers really come into their own in dirty water. In fact, huge trout that seldom feed during the day can be approached and caught on a fly because they lose their normal caution. Minnows and crayfish get pushed around, disoriented, and swept into deeper water, and trout respond to this with a vengeance. Streamers are big enough to be spotted by trout in dirty water, and a bright pattern, something with white or yellow in it, can often draw strikes in water that seems to dirty for fly fishing. If you happen to be on the river during a quick rise of water after a rainstorm, the first hour after the water gets dirty can provide some amazing streamer fishing.

Low, clear water, where current flow is restricted to a narrow thread, presents other challenges and opportunities. In big rivers, trout that might be difficult to reach, even with your longest cast, can be approached (but with caution). It's also easier to read the water during low flows because water that has enough current to provide food is limited to places where you see the line of bubbles and debris weaving its way through a pool. Fish that were spread out over hundreds of feet during higher flows may now be confined to a narrow slot.

Low flows also offer better dry-fly fishing. At higher velocities, trout are reluctant to move toward the surface because it's too much work, and they get pushed out of position by the current. However, as the current slows, trout can hover just below the surface, sipping insects from the film with little effort. Typically, this calls for a cautious, straight upstream approach and a small fly. A beetle, ant, or midge pattern will often do the trick.

It's often possible to see trout in low water, a luxury you don't have in most rivers because the trout are too deep and well camouflaged to locate. But when the sun is overhead during low water, you will be able to see some of them. Fishing for a trout you can see in shallow water with a small nymph is one of the greatest thrills in flyfishing. You must approach the fish from directly downstream or you'll spook it. And you must use a long leader, at least a 12-footer, and remove any weight and strike indicators from the leader. Pitch a lightly weighted nymph ahead of the fish. A good rule of thumb is to lead the fish by double its depth; in other words, if a trout is lying in a foot of water, lead it by two. You may see your leader twitch as the fish takes the fly, but most anglers watch the fish instead of the leader. If the fish moves to the side or seems to dart after something when your fly is even with its position, make one quick strip of line. If the trout hasn't eaten your fly, it might think that the bug has suddenly put on speed;

if it has, then you're in business! Striking by raising the rod tip will usually spook the fish.

FOOD-RICH VERSUS FOOD-POOR STREAMS

Knowing the relative density of trout and the abundance of food in a river can shortcut a lot of trial and error in approach and presentation. Brown trout in a sterile mountain stream can appear to be different animals than their counterparts in a rich tailwater river. You may know something about the richness of the river you're fishing already, from reading about it or talking to other people on the river. But even if it's an unknown stream in a Wisconsin cornfield, there are ways you can eyeball a river to get some clues.

Rich streams look soupy. They often have some type of aquatic vegetation, either rooted to the bottom, along the banks, or clinging to rocks. The water may be clear, but the bottom will probably not look clean because of all the organic matter. Stable rivers (typically tailwater rivers and spring creeks) seldom flood, and don't have wide gravel banks. Instead, vegetation grows right down to the water's edge, because it is not uprooted by frequent periods of high, fast water. This stability encourages trout and

Wide rocky banks, clear water, and no submerged vegetation tell you the trout in this river won't be too picky about fly patterns.

insect growth. Streams in lowlands are typically richer than mountain streams, because they pick up nutrients as they flow.

Food-poor streams look clean or tea-stained. Streams with clean rocks and clear water don't have an abundance of organic matter. Nor do tea-stained rivers, because this tinge comes from acidic soils, usually heavy in conifers. Acidic streams, with a pH of less than 7.0, are limited in insect life, and almost devoid of crustaceans, because the dissolved calcium needed to grow a crustacean's shell is very low in acidic streams. Wide gravel or rock banks indicate strong water fluctuations during the season, which further reduce a river's productivity.

Examples of food-rich streams include most of the West's famous tailwaters, such as Montana's Bighorn, Madison, and Missouri; New Mexico's San Juan; Colorado's South Platte; Utah's Green; and California's Pit. The White River in Arkansas is a food-rich tailwater, as is New York's Delaware. All of the famous spring creeks, from Hat Creek in California to Montana's Paradise Valley creeks to Pennsylvania's Letort and Falling Springs are rich in food. It's harder to give you famous examples of food-poor streams, because by nature they don't produce huge fish or large numbers of them and are thus not as popular. New York's Ausable, Wisconsin's Brule, Montana's Kootenai, and nearly all small mountain streams fall into the food-poor category. Many rivers, like Vermont's Battenkill, New York's Beaverkill, Pennsylvania's Kettle Creek, and Wyoming's Snake, fall into a middle-of-the-road category, for which predictions are tough.

Trout in food-rich streams will be more selective about what they eat. They may eat during spurts of insect abundance rather than all day long, and won't grab every piece of food that drifts past. Your fishing day might consist of hours of slow periods followed by intense feeding activity. They won't move far for their food, so casting accuracy is more important. Blind fishing a dry fly is seldom productive except during the summer, when grasshoppers, beetles, and ants can be effective in the middle of the day. If you don't see any hatches, a nymph fished dead drift will be your most reliable method. Streamers work best at dawn and dusk, but can also be effective tossed right up against a deep bank.

Trout can be found anywhere in food-rich streams. Reading the water in this kind of river is tough, because each river seems to have its idiosyncrasy when it comes to what kind of water fish prefer. They can often be found in almost-stagnant backwaters, because food is abundant even there, and it's easier for them to capture food in the slow currents. Fish all types of water and look for rises in unexpected places. Once you find some fish, stay there and fish thoroughly, because they often form pods and many trout can be packed into one place, all feeding at once.

Where trout have an abundance of food, they are not as easy to frighten. Apparently the stimulus of getting as much food as possible overrides their caution. In some of these rich streams trout will even follow anglers through riffles, feeding right at their feet on insects kicked up during wading. Thus, you can confidently fish a pool that another angler has just left, and if you spook a rising fish, sit on the bank for a few minutes because it will probably resume feeding. Also, keep in mind that on popular rivers, where trout are used to seeing anglers all day, the fish can actually get conditioned to your presence and not view you as a threat.

In food-poor streams, on the other hand, trout don't see large quantities of any one insect. They are seldom selective except during the rare hatch. They feed eagerly all day long, as long as the water temperature is between 50 and 65°F. You can fish nearly any kind of fly with success, including dry flies, even if no rises are seen. Flies as large as a Size 10 can be effective, even if none of the insects you see are that large. Wet flies swung in the current, and even twitched or dragging dry flies, can be effective. Your strategy here should be to catch a trout's attention.

Trout in these streams will only be in prime spots—places where slow water meets the main current, heads and tails of pools, right next to rocks and logs, and along deep banks. There is not enough drifting food to support them in slower backwaters. Each spot may only have one or two fish in it, and the fish will either grab your fly or spook. Move often and don't waste much time in each pool.

Trout here will be more easily frightened. They are not preoccupied with feeding and are constantly on the alert. Even though you should not spend much time in each pool, don't rush up and down the banks. If you spook a trout, forget it, as that fish might not feed again for hours. For the same reason, try to avoid fishing water that has been occupied recently by another angler, because this water will be spoiled for longer than even the most patient angler is willing to wait.

10

ETIQUETTE

I'M NOT GOING TO PREACH TO YOU. I believe that most boorish behavior on trout streams is due to ignorance and inexperience. Good anglers know that unfished water is more productive because the fish have not been frightened, so they avoid pools and runs that are occupied by other anglers. They seek out places in a river that may not be as popular, because they know they can find fresh trout that are more likely to take a fly.

Try to put maximum distance between yourself and other anglers. If a river is uncrowded, find a pool that is empty. Try to find a place where you can't see another person. You may not care about solitude but they might. If you can't stay out of sight, at least try to position yourself at the other end of a pool or riffle.

If a river is too wide or deep to wader across, it's okay to fish across from another angler as long as the person on the other side can't reach the water on your side, even with a long cast. You might ask if the person across from you minds if you fish on your side. If you see an angler sitting on the bank next to a piece of water, he might be waiting for a hatch or spinner fall. That person should be accorded the same respect as if he were actively fishing the water.

Finally, it's in your best interest to treat private land with respect, which means asking for permission, cleaning up your litter and anyone else's, and closing pasture gates behind you. Inconsiderate behavior gets land posted.

INDEX